Library and Information Service

Library materials must be returned on or before the last date stamped or fines will be charged at the current rate. Items can be renewed by telephone, letter or personal call unless required by another borrower. For hours of opening and charges see notices displayed in libraries.

First published in 2009 by
Franklin Watts
338 Euston Road
London
NW1 3BH

Franklin Watts Australia
Level 17/207 Kent Street
Sydney
NSW 2000

A CIP catalogue record for this book is available
from the British Library.

ISBN 978 0 7496 8373 3 (hbk)
ISBN 978 0 7496 8379 5 (pbk)

Series Editor: Melanie Palmer
Series Advisor: Dr Barrie Wade
Series Designer: Peter Scoulding
Consultant: Professor Ghulam Sarwar

Printed in China

Franklin Watts is a division of
Hachette Children's Books,
an Hachette Livre UK company
www.hachettelivre.co.uk

The Flight from Makkah

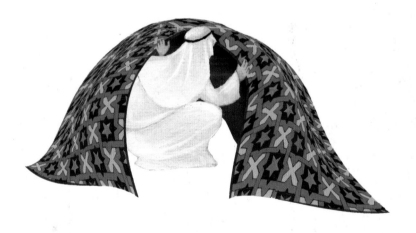

by Anita Ganeri and Serena Curmi

W
FRANKLIN WATTS
LONDON • SYDNEY

About this book

The story of the Flight from Makkah comes from the religion of Islam. Islam began in the Middle East about 1,400 years ago. Muslims (followers of Islam) believe that Allah (God) sent a series of prophets to teach people how to live. The last and greatest of these was Muhammad (Peace Be Upon Him*). Muhammad (PBUH) was born in the city of Makkah in Arabia (modern-day Saudi Arabia) in about 570 CE. *The Flight from Makkah* tells how he escaped from people plotting his death and fled to Madinah in 622 CE. His journey is known as the *hijrah* (flight).

* This is abbreviated to PBUH after the first mention. Following Islamic tradition, the illustrations in this book do not show faces of people or depictions of Allah or Muhammad (PBUH).

For many years, the Prophet
Muhammad (Peace Be Upon Him)
lived in the city of Makkah.

Muhammad (PBUH) taught people about Allah, and many people became Muslims like him.

But the rich merchants of Makkah were afraid of losing their power if people worshipped Allah.

Allah told Muhammad (PBUH) to leave Makkah and travel to the city of Madinah.

The merchants were plotting to kill Muhammad (PBUH). They did not want him in their city.

The angel Jibril warned
Muhammad (PBUH) about
the merchants' wicked plan.

So Muhammad's (PBUH) cousin, Ali, slept in Muhammad's (PBUH) bed instead. The merchants were furious when they found out.

Meanwhile, Muhammad (PBUH)
and his friend Abu Bakr
quickly escaped.

They set off on two camels,
on the long journey across
the desert to Madinah.

Muhammad (PBUH) and his friend
Abu rode fast, but the merchants
were not far behind them.

Just then Muhammad (PBUH) and Abu saw a cave. They knew that Allah would keep them safe there.

From the cave, they heard the merchants. Their voices got louder as they rode nearer.

"Over there! A cave!" said one merchant. "Maybe they're hiding inside it. Let's look!"

"'No one's been here for years," said another merchant. "Look, the entrance is covered with cobwebs."

The merchants could not find Muhammad (PBUH) so they gave up their search and went home.

Inside the cave, Muhammad (PBUH) and Abu Bakr were filled with relief. They were safe at last.

"Where did those cobwebs come from?" asked Abu Bakr. "They weren't there before."

Muhammad (PBUH) smiled at his
friend. He knew that Allah had
been watching over them.

The two men stayed in the cave for a while to make sure that they were safe.

Then they set off once more across the desert sands on their long and thirsty journey.

They rode all through the night, when it was cooler, and rested during the heat of the day.

News of Muhammad's (PBUH) journey from Makkah had already reached the people of Madinah.

Every day, they went to the edge
of the city and waited eagerly
for him to arrive.

At last, Muhammad (PBUH) and Abu Bakr reached Madinah. They were given a great welcome.

Many people invited Muhammad (PBUH) to stay in their houses. But the Prophet waited until his camel stopped to decide where to stay.

Finally, his camel rested near the house of Abu Ayyub Ansari. Muhammad (PBUH) stayed in the house for a few days.

Then he built a mosque and a house to live in, and brought great joy to the people of Madinah.

Hopscotch has been specially designed to fit the requirements of the Literacy Framework. It offers real books by top authors and illustrators for children developing their reading skills.

ADVENTURES

Aladdin and the Lamp
ISBN 978 0 7496 6692 7

Blackbeard the Pirate
ISBN 978 0 7496 6690 3

George and the Dragon
ISBN 978 0 7496 6691 0

Jack the Giant-Killer
ISBN 978 0 7496 6693 4

TALES OF KING ARTHUR

1. The Sword in the Stone
ISBN 978 0 7496 6694 1

2. Arthur the King
ISBN 978 0 7496 6695 8

3. The Round Table
ISBN 978 0 7496 6697 2

4. Sir Lancelot and the Ice Castle
ISBN 978 0 7496 6698 9

TALES OF ROBIN HOOD

Robin and the Knight
ISBN 978 0 7496 6699 6

Robin and the Monk
ISBN 978 0 7496 6700 9

Robin and the Silver Arrow
ISBN 978 0 7496 6703 0

Robin and the Friar
ISBN 978 0 7496 6702 3

FAIRY TALES

The Emperor's New Clothes
ISBN 978 0 7496 7421 2

Cinderella
ISBN 978 0 7496 7417 5

Snow White
ISBN 978 0 7496 7418 2

Jack and the Beanstalk
ISBN 978 0 7496 7422 9

The Three Billy Goats Gruff
ISBN 978 0 7496 7420 5

The Pied Piper of Hamelin
ISBN 978 0 7496 7419 9

Goldilocks and the Three Bears
ISBN 978 0 7496 7903 3

Hansel and Gretel
ISBN 978 0 7496 7904 0

The Three Little Pigs
ISBN 978 0 7496 7905 7

Rapunzel
ISBN 978 0 7496 7906 4

Little Red Riding Hood
ISBN 978 0 7496 7907 1

Rumpelstiltskin
ISBN 978 0 7496 7908 8

HISTORIES

Toby and the Great Fire of London
ISBN 978 0 7496 7410 6

Pocahontas the Peacemaker
ISBN 978 0 7496 7411 3

Grandma's Seaside Bloomers
ISBN 978 0 7496 7412 0

Hoorah for Mary Seacole
ISBN 978 0 7496 7413 7

Remember the 5th of November
ISBN 978 0 7496 7414 4

Tutankhamun and the Golden Chariot
ISBN 978 0 7496 7415 1

MYTHS

Icarus, the Boy Who Flew
ISBN 978 0 7496 7992 7 *
ISBN 978 0 7496 8000 8

Perseus and the Snake Monster
ISBN 978 0 7496 7993 4 *
ISBN 978 0 7496 8001 5

Odysseus and the Wooden Horse
ISBN 978 0 7496 7994 1 *
ISBN 978 0 7496 8002 2

Persephone and the Pomegranate Seeds
ISBN 978 0 7496 7995 8 *
ISBN 978 0 7496 8003 9

Romulus and Remus
ISBN 978 0 7496 7996 5 *
ISBN 978 0 7496 8004 6

Thor's Hammer
ISBN 978 0 7496 7997 2*
ISBN 978 0 7496 8005 3

No Dinner for Anansi
ISBN 978 0 7496 7998 9 *
ISBN 978 0 7496 8006 0

Gelert the Brave
ISBN 978 0 7496 7999 6*
ISBN 978 0 7496 8007 7

STORIES OF RELIGION

The Good Samaritan
ISBN 978 0 7496 8369 6*
ISBN 978 0 7496 8375 7

The Loaves and the Fishes
ISBN 978 0 7496 8370 2*
ISBN 978 0 7496 8376 4

The Prince and Holika the Witch
ISBN 978 0 7496 8371 9*
ISBN 978 0 7496 8377 1

The Birth of Krishna
ISBN 978 0 7496 8368 9 *
ISBN 978 0 7496 8374 0

The Flight from Makkah
ISBN 978 0 7496 8373 3*
ISBN 978 0 7496 8379 5

The Great Night Journey
ISBN 978 0 7496 8372 6*
ISBN 978 0 7496 8378 8

For more details go to:
www.franklinwatts.co.uk

* **hardback**